**He is before all things, and in him
all things hold together.**

Colossians 1:17

For Morgan and Sandy

Poem Salt

Published by:
Powder River Publishing LLC
1014 Black Mountain Road
Thermopolis, Wyoming 82443

Copyright © 2023
ISBN: 978-1-956881-39-4
Printed in the United States of America

Powder River Publishing

www.powderriverpublishing.com

Table of contents

I.

The Pietà

The controlled burn of her heart
stops just short of killing her,
pushes through screams
muffled by a stillness
so brutal a nearby olive tree
loses consciousness.
The flaming universe
has a fire break now,
a smoldering path of hope—
nettles and brambles, cleared.
One of her delicate, pale hands
holds her son's torn corpse,
the other waits
for the wind to pick-up speed.

*The inspiration for this ekphrastic poem is Michelangelo's sculpture, Madonna della Pietà, circa 1498-9.

At the Busy Bee Cafe Where I Spot Sugar Plums in the Abyss

The sounds I hear in the wee hours
aren't the Celtic whispers of Irish ancestors
overlapped by house crackles and crickets,
but the profoundly useless grind of my mind
trying to rewrite the evening news
in iambic pentameter.

"Sacred texts burn as easily as Dr. Seuss"
my atheist friend, Helen, says over lunch,
an offhand remark
that strikes me harder than she knows,
cognizant as I am
of how far we have evolved
from the ability to memorize.

Success and honor changed course
without asking, are pretending
to have been enacted into law as birthrights
that require nothing but
a good wifi connection and a selfie stick.

Nothing new about senators
holding journalists instead of history books,
but day by day

the streets seem a little riskier,
dotted with lost people
wanting to touch something,
but they don't know what it is.

Some of us try to padlock our gates
with relative innocence,
but we aren't quite sure what that is, either.

Somebody in the kitchen
is getting rough with the dishes.

Now Helen is telling me
about her new furniture,
Natuzzi Italia, and a faint
"If I could just find a way to get rid of that cat . . ."
is the last thing I hear

because I'm thinking about the saints,
how they knew they weren't such
because they were perfect,
but because they could see their own sin
so clearly it made them bleed.

Yesterday I quietly slid my list of topics
it's still okay to talk about
into the big garbage can in the garage.

Yet, compassion is everywhere.
I can see it through the cafe window,
piled by the side of the road,
dangling from clouds,
clinging to that UPS guy's shoe.

3

Lizards in the Castle

They slip-in through cracks in the foundation.

Sometimes during morning prayer

fear and trust trade chairs.

My spirit stops running,

stands straight-up and turns around,

looks directly into the beady eyes,

and hideous, razor-toothed faces

of St.Teresa's reptiles.

This is where they stop laughing,

start backing towards the door.

Nobody is more surprised than me.

I don't know where they go

or who they talk to in the afternoon,

only that they'll be back.

Where Did All the Fiddles Go?

Old man Baker is dead.
Cowboy, musician, comedian.
Salt.

Baker had a new iphone.
Far be it from me to hint
that Facebook drove him to do
what he did a week ago today.
Never mind what Sam at the feed store thinks.

But Baker's violin, she hangs
here in his cabin.
Loose strings, and pegs,
a thick wrap of dust
spread across her shoulders.
An old woman down for the count.
Hushed, like Baker before he . . . you know.

She must think nobody wants her.
She must think no one even remembers
the schottische and waltz melodies
that rang from her belly
during family reunions at Magpie Creek.

The people danced.

My son caught his first fish.
Dirty-faced bands of kids

in boots and crumpled hats
darted around the denim legs of cowboys.

People danced.

Skittish barn cats. Green Jell-o salad.
Beef brisket, border collies, and tadpoles in a jar.
Laughter, shortbread cookies,
squabbles over who said what
would rise, then fall,

and the people danced.

I can't stand the way this grieving fiddle
just hangs here.
I grab her by the neck,
force her to look at me.

"The people danced, didn't they?" I said

No response.

"Breathe," I tell her. "Please."

I glance out the window and back.
I tell her the prairie is still here.
I tell her memories of the thing aren't the thing.

She shrugs.

Nothing to do but leave this place.
I like how she hums and twangs a little
when we step out into the wind.

Dog Envy in the Tower of Babel

Yesterday I saw a stray dog at the park.
He peed on the mailbox near the chokecherry,
then wagged and greeted me
without expressing a single political opinion.

He doesn't wonder
if the mailbox ever gets confused,
just standing there, unable to do anything
but hold other people's stories,
and watch cars go by.

I admit to a flash of jealousy
at his lack of need to know
what the road thinks of him,
or if the half a ham sandwich
he ate by the dumpster was full of ants.
He wolfed that thing down like he was
100% sure it had been made up to code.

I don't think he even noticed
that the conservative ham had rotted,
the liberal mayo had grown toxic in the sun.
He just flat doesn't give a damn.

Not like me. A clanging washing machine,
banging around about the need to shift its weight . . .

> Something's not right
> > Something's not right
> > > Something's not right

7

Compassion

There isn't a warning beforehand.
The empty suitcase of your heart
doesn't know a trip is coming up.
That it will, for a moment,
be stuffed with a compassion
that will push on the hinges.
Sometimes we forget how interchangeable
compassion and love are,
how one can bleed into the other
until only God can sort the whole thing out.

There's a fierce, pounding rain
in downtown Cheyenne,
like the kind you see in Texas.
It washes away piles
of marble size hail lining the street.
The stoplight has quit working.

Cars sit balled-up
in that uncomfortable place
where you know the system
is on the blink,
but haven't quite decided
how much risk you're willing to take
to keep moving forward.

He might be homeless, that grizzled old man

standing on the corner.
His denim jacket is torn and soiled.
It's too big.
He could use a shave, maybe a few teeth.
He wears the prerequisite hobo's hat.
A handmade, wooden flute dangles
by a leather cord
from the waistband of his pants.
Behind him, a modified backpack of sorts.
He has pulled the front of his coat
around a lump on his chest,
shields it with both palms.

The timid face of a drowned rat
pokes its soaked head out the V
at the neck of his jacket.
No, wait. It's a puppy.

FOLLOW ME HE SAID

In my dream
it's a narrow trail
that leads up
and winds around
a mountain that rises
out of nowhere.
I don't recognize
this species of evergreen tree,
and I don't know
how I got here.
The trail is skinny
and my feet are huge.
There's a sheer cliff
to my right, and at the bottom,
a bunch of friends
sit on a creek bank,
starving to death
for lack of hope.
Their own words
don't comfort them anymore.
I want to stop and help,
but they yell
"You're just dreaming!"
and wave me on by.

A vine that I've known
for a long time
drops into my path
and I grab on.
It swings me
toward a tunnel
that has a bright light
at the far end,
so I let go
and make a mad run
towards the glow
because I'm not
as stupid as I look,
but the alarm clock
on my iPhone
pulls me back
to the furnace kicking on,
the sound of the doggie door
in the kitchen, closing.

The Horses are Making a Run for it

The librarian wants to know
if the poem I'm going to read the preschool group
has a horse in it.

"Well, no," I say. "It only has winter in it."

She tells me everything will be about horses today,
and lets her declaration hang in the air,
as if my personal, overdone, winter theme
is a topic that is technically dead,
but still moving.
Half a snake. A headless chicken.

"I know one about a llama," I tell her.
"Horses," she said.

I lay my poem on the puzzle table
and begin to peruse the children's section
where I pull a staggering array of equine verse,
but not a single one does justice
to how cold the mornings are breaking,

how there has been a wild wind at my back
trying to push me out a corral gate,

for long years whispering a hum of guidance
I can't make out. Something about the need
to bring my whole contraption down—
the pulleys and the winch,
life-jackets, balaclavas, and hydraulic lifts,
rescue chains, and chamomile tea.

I've never known when to stop
busting snow drifts in knee-high mukluks,
waving a flaming torch,
desperate to herd my people to safety,
pushing flank along the softer trails
around battlefields, poverty, and black ice—
dodging sink holes, and man-eating plants,
snollygosters, and wolves-in-wool.

But the herd keeps getting away.

Memories in the Mirror Are Closer Than They Appear

Thirty below and the sewer is sluggish,
so I flush and plunge and flush,
prop the cupboard doors open,
get the fire going.

I try to force warm thoughts
through the pipes,
pushing them underground across the yard
to the main connection on the street.

Of course it won't help,
but when your power is limited
it's good to give your mind a job
so it won't start freezing to things.

And you said I was useless. Ha.

A Cautionary Tale For Beginners

Leah used to think attachment was a good thing
so she became a barnacle.

Stuck herself to lampposts and mailboxes.
Her attachments had a gluttonous quality,

and she would eat things
like paintings of moonlight loitering on lakes.

Washed them down with beads of water
licked from her grandmother's umbrella.

In her living room she built an altar
with boards, and cinder blocks,

and a candle that glowed
upon every object her children had ever touched.

She ate the plaster-of-Paris handprints,
and the small jars of dry bean soup

with yarn tied in a bow around the lids.
She ate the pretty rocks, the paper hearts.

The candlelight, trying to save itself,
clung to hot blobs of dripping wax.

Homeless dogs followed her everywhere.
She ate them. Said to her friends,

"Run. Hide in the forest," and they did.
She is old now, with no appetite.

She watches European movies with subtitles.
The words make a brief appearance, then leave.

More words come. Then go.
She says the characters don't eat much.

There's always a quiet old man or woman,
sweeping something in the background.

Happiness

The horizon performs its whole big prairie ado,
rolling consciousness over hill after hill
below a sky busy making promises it can't keep,
(I'm the limit, really,)
but above indifferent mats of cacti, jagged cutbanks,
and the occasional abandoned tire.
Horizon, oracle of mixed messages,
hosting reality's slight-of-hand
across what appears to be
a beautifully lit stretch of happiness—
calm as a coffee bean rosary.

Careful.

A wise person will be suspicious.
Even I can see the serrated edges on every sunset.

Poem With No Lantern

If a man wishes to be sure of the road
he's traveling on, then he must close
his eyes and travel in the dark.
—St. John of the Cross

I wasted too much time

trying to focus my eyes

on the celestial opera

of my own divinations.

Not a one can make the trip.

All they do is whine

and ask where the bathroom is.

I stuffed them into a shoebox

and sent them down Powder River

on a cardboard raft.

Best to stop here

for the night.

I stretch myself out

in the grassy half-pipe

of a thirsty irrigation ditch.

Facedown. Still.

Ah. There it is.

The sound of the wind
carrying prayers
from one side of the world
to the other.

The Situation is Thus

Poems roll and foam like the evening tide

that nightly pulls back a layer of sand,

exposes abandoned shells and shark eyes.

Sometimes there's a rotted log with a cricket inside,

throwing his sound around a quiet beach.

There are ghost tales of lighthouse watchmen

who think they hear something at sea, calling.

And pirate ships, docked, thieves leaving their den.

Some stories start on the ocean floor,

crawling along the bottom like sonar.

When the fog lifts, neap tide's full of poem salt.

Mercifully, the words have been washed away.

Yet here I sit, both arms wrapped around the wind.

Somebody needs to get a life.

Anchors

Sea, claw, auger, hinged,

fixed shank scoop,

body, blood, prayer, faith,

hope, love, forgiveness.

Better late than never.

If someone had thought

to give me this list in childhood,

(before I had to try to make my own)

God would not have had

to raise his voice so often.

Later, I didn't share it enough.

So here, take it. Stop drifting.

The angels get seasick.

Wings

Aircraft, bird, dragonfly, bee,

body, blood, prayer, faith,

hope, love, forgiveness.

I read about a monk

who lived in a cold cave

on the side of a mountain.

I suppose he didn't want distractions.

One can only guess

how he used spare time

when he wasn't praying

for the rest of us.

Maybe he napped, dreamed of wings.

Feathers are good insulation.

Not to mention useful for flying

down the steep face of a cliff

to help a lost traveler,

or grab a few wild strawberries,

or maybe, just maybe, to soar high like an eagle.

The Good Thief

There is no escape from the flies on his cheek.

They look him in the eye and tell him

This is as good as it gets for the likes of you,

so relax, settle-in for eternity.

A disembodied moan evaporates

into the ether like moisture rising off

blood-stained sheets flapping on a clothesline.

A spectator coughs. A baby's brief cry.

Confession rises from unbidden nowhere.

Repentance comes for him, hammer and tongs.

He is too weak to resist the emptying,

or the osmosis that quietly follows

like blue sky filling the mouth of a cave.

So that's what love looks like, **he whispers.**

Jesus, remember me . . .

The Red Siren at the Edge of the Park

A siren blasts at noon each Wednesday sharp,
a test good fortune calls unpopular,
the town reminded maybe something hard,
unseen, is touching soft our jugulars.

We jump at first, then glance at kids on swings.
My friend Eva's cancer holds her present,
like riding blind a horse that slips and springs.
Ah, hope, your rash so fine and violent

amidst the doom that catches breath at night.
By dawn we aim our joy at precipice
and shoot, we stars in glitzy dresses bright,
our dancing twinkle dying, credulous,

right in Reaper's face. Life is short. I flay
my timid flinch. It yelps and slinks away.

The Dental Hygienist Scrapes My Teeth With a Description of Her Cuban Vacation

"They are always laughing,
can you believe that?
Nothing but old cars,
they just keep fixing them.

"All the buildings need work,
crumbling stucco, peeling paint.
Tin roofs blow off, you know.
No one seems to care.

"Music is a big deal.
A little Afro-Cuban jazz
goes a long way if you ask me.

"Your gums are receding. Massage, okay?

"The law says no doggie-bags
can leave the cafe, someone
might be getting extra *congri*.

If you lie and say it's for your dog
you might get away with it.

"Our tour guide said they recycle everything.
Water glasses are the cut bottoms of rum bottles.

"You flinched, did that hurt? Sorry.

"They use shower curtains for doors.
I can't imagine why the kids are so happy.

"You never know
when the guy standing in front of you
is going to start singing.
Everyone gets twenty dollars a month.

"I can tell you don't want me
in your mouth. I'll hurry.

"Not much to buy in Havana,
so if you want to shop forget it.
Our cab driver was a neurosurgeon.

"Everyone knows how to dance,
on the sidewalks, in the streets.
At first I thought they were being swarmed
by bees or something.

"No one is allowed to get ahead.

"What's wrong with those people?
Festivals all over the place.
I'll never go back."

Casual Observations

Sometimes I mistake them for angels,

sometimes I think

they are simply flashes

of crude, imaginary insights

caught on the arbitrary camera

of my peripheral vision,

sent by no one

to change nothing.

Still, I write them down.

Vaque descriptions,

like the lady standing beside me

at the grocery store yesterday,

squeezing avocados—

her kind remark about my hair,

how I teared up.

Bedtime in a Crowded Room

I fluff my pillow, flip it to the cool side before opening the rear door of my mind. They've been waiting in a tidy, single file line and as everyone enters, I kiss my grandmother's cheek, straighten my grandfather's collar. My mother takes an unapproved liberty right-off, stumbles over a pile of books as she tries to beat my father to his favorite seat next to the emergency exit. Here comes the almost lover whose plane didn't see the mountain until it was too late, and the old man who, notwithstanding poor vision and hearing, thought I was a saint. And the kid from high school, who tried to vacuum-up a spilled pitcher of Kool-Aid, and the neighbor with emphysema who begged me to place a plastic bag over his head and hold his wrists. A roll of duct tape sat on the table by his chair, in case I changed my mind. Next up, the best friend who drowned in the Colorado River, diving drunk into a most wicked undertow. I have trundle beds in my head for Maria and Egyptian, the little kids at my volunteer job who had AIDS before the pediatric cocktail, and who taught me that it's possible to live happily with anything. Anything at all. The bed bounces. My god, so many dogs—who by the way, still get to sleep wherever they damn well please.

Snow Falling Down and Piling-Up Like Bad Poetry

Steam on the cafe window, I use my sleeve.

Outside, snowdrifts spread their confusions

into the road on sharp missiles of wind

aimed across the prairie, speed reading

intermittent sentences of rabbitbush and barbed wire.

There will be no figuring it out. Life.

Sometimes the mind wonders

if it might all be a massive hallucination,

beautiful and grotesque at the same time.

I waste a lot of energy sewing words

that try to button the whole thing up.

Most of them start out trying to describe

Love and Truth,

but Love yaks on and on about flying shoes,

while Truth just sits there looking stupid

with a basket of mysteries in its lap.

Every so often it looks up and asks me

if anyone else is writing this down.

"No offense," it'll say.

A tea kettle whistles in the kitchen.

Time and Chance

Even if I filled the yard
with apes and peacocks
and fourteen hundred chariots,
ate the healthiest food,
hit the gym three times a week
and hiked ten miles on the off days,
became rich, or poor, ugly, or beautiful—
it ends. I wasted too much time
navigating the wrong world.
Vanity of vanities . . ., the wise man said.
It's not like we haven't been warned.
King Solomon sits at my kitchen table,
sips a cup of Tulsi tea.
"I told you so," he said.

Shhh

I turn the car off, close the garage door

to shut the world out. It's hard to move.

The voice coming from my iPhone podcast

speaks of a container full of dead babies,

unceremoniously delivered

to a recycle center from a D.C. abortion clinic.

No one is supposed to think

too hard about this.

A plane passes overhead.

Its deceptively gentle hum

filters through the roof shingles.

Could be a squadron of crop dusters,

circling around and around,

spraying fogs of cowardice onto the masses.

The Only One

The sun rises yet again, this time

letting one large cloud take the credit

by absorbing more than its share

of magenta light, but only for a moment.

Nobody gets to keep it for long.

Leaning over the porch rail in my bathrobe,

I watch the wild bees

in their shiny, neon green helmets, sleeping,

curled around cool spears of Agastache.

Without a mirror,

an eye can't see the face it lives in.

I'm guessing each bee probably thinks

she's the only one who doesn't have

a beautiful little metallic head that lights up.

The Ghost of Leonard Cohen Leans on the Doorframe While I Try to Get the Lid Off the Honey

"It's all good," he said.

"No need for sarcasm," I said.

When hot water doesn't work,

bang it on the counter.

Maybe someone will hear

and come to help.

If nobody turns around,

and there is no sweet in your tea,

you will have to do without.

Or, you can just eat the whole thing, jar and all.

Your choice. And don't worry.

You-know-who will catch up with you later,

after the glass has shredded your tongue.

Hallelujah.

Rethinking an Innocent Omission While Accompanying My Friend to the Doctor

His office is a heretofore
never-seen-in-nature green.
I fully expect to hear birds
burst into song any minute now.
Fluorescent lights flicker, click,
disturb the rain forest atmosphere.

I can't help but stare
at Dr. Kendrick's fingers
as they dart across the keyboard.
First thing Wednesday morning
they'll be working
inside my friend Mary's abdomen.

Images settle on the computer screen,
flashes of behind-the-scenes activity
in the City of Mary.
It doesn't seem right somehow,

Kendrick's impatient racing
through fuzzy black and white scans
of Mary's main drag,
passing a church, a liquor store,
the Chamber of Commerce, and a car wash.

His annoyed, eye-twitching expression
is that of a man
who wants to find a five-star hotel,
but all he can see is a fleabag, ramshackle dive
with a neon MEDICARE sign blinking above it,
elderly street walkers haunting the corner
of Hip and Spine—their faces lit
fuchsia, yellow, fuchsia, yellow again.
My cousin Cami is the surgeon's housekeeper.
She tells me things.
Last week at Bingo she said this steel sliver of a man
spends his solitary evenings listening to Yo Yo Ma
and preening a pride of Himalayan cats.

"Sometimes he drools and dangles a little live mouse
over their heads, then smiles
when they bat it with their paws,
right before they, well, you know," she said.
Cami isn't reliable.

Later that night Mary asked

"What did Cami have to say about him?"

I may have mentioned something

about the good doctor being a music lover.

Nah, Looks Like a Whale to Me

My sister and brother and I
used to watch the skies
for cloud figures, as if being
the first one to spot
the lion, donkey, or ballerina
was a sign of personal genius.

Never mind that one person's horse
is another person's ogre.
But I'm sure God uses clouds
like he uses everything else.
No telling what signs I've missed.

He probably shows his face plenty.
If we looked up more often,
we might catch him
rolling his eyes, grinding his teeth,
especially when he hears us
telling ourselves how we
are doing the best we can.
"Ew," we say when a flash of insight

brings a gangrenous blemish
to the fore of our conscience,

mere seconds before we pat ourself on the back
for having noticed it at all.
You'd think with our track record,
we would simply forfeit the point
as too redundant to warrant applause.
Not a chance.
We take it, alright,
lead with it and others like it
every time the need for healing
tries to distract us from our heroism.

Even so, minute progression continues,
albeit, at the rate of a snail
trying to cross an ocean
of crushed beach glass,
dragging trails of mucous
over light's persistent glint.

A Spring Reminder

Two house finches built a nest
on the eye-level, dead Christmas wreath
hanging by my front door.
Opportunists, those two.

The male with his flashing red face,
the female, plain, only her mission flashing.
Twigs, grass, the cottony end of a Q-tip, a bread tie.

She filled a three-egg-size nest
with five eggs and settled in.

The big hatch was an occasion.
Birds all over the place.
Five triangular faces begged through a curtain
of dry spruce and a giant red bow.

I checked every morning, expecting
a naked nestling knocked aside,
flopping on the porch,
no one to help her but me
and my natural draw to no-win situations.

The parents spent their time hunting,
feeding, and chirping obscenities
from the honeylocust tree
as I went about spring yard clean-up.

This morning the kids fled upon my arrival.
Up and away, 1, 2, 3, 4, 5. One at a time,
as if connected by an invisible thread,
flying like pros.

Head feathers are still new,
jutting-out at goofball angles,
making them look like
a little flock of fools.

The yard is quiet and sad.
I pull the wreath down.

There it is. The mess.
I'm not going to complain, though.
Jesus has to do this all the time.

The Deacon's Dog

A one-eyed dog lives
in a large yard behind the church.
Deacon Sam said she wandered in one day
and wouldn't leave.
Some sort of shepherd cross, he thinks.
He tried to get her story
while doctoring the wound
where the skin on her neck had surrendered
to a collar of knotted baling twine and maggots,
but she didn't want to talk about it.

He even told her about Clare,
the icy road, the drunk driver,
how hard is forgiveness,
how there was a time
he didn't think he could do it,
how a thing called grace helped.

She listened, but still wouldn't talk.
Sam let her stay. Calls her Gracie.
The enclosure is her whole world. She owns it.
Growls and bares her teeth when someone walks by.

Best not to make eye contact.

At least the yard produces predictable phenomena—
a bowl of food every morning,
wild turkeys that roost in the ponderosa pines,
a tender-hearted priest who accidentally
lobs a donut over the chainlink every Sunday.

There are dragons in town,
but they stay on the other side of the fence.
Even better, they startle when she hits the wire.

The squirrels say she's crazy.

Sam reads her a poem every night at bedtime.
Robert Frost, Wendell Berry, that sort of thing.
Afterwards, she stretches way down
into that cold, empty space at his back.
She stays close so his scars
won't wiggle in the dark.

While Sam sleeps,
Gracie keeps an ear out for dragons.

The Most Important Job in the World

I see through her sliding glass door,

early every day as I walk my dog,

before the morning light

has cast its hopeful ray

onto a single blade of grass.

The old woman sits in her living room,

a tattered cloth recliner chair

and its dingy, off-white brocade pattern,

an obese yellow cat always asleep on her lap.

An aluminum walker waits at her knees,

a plain wooden cane leans on the chair,

both part of an intricate network of aids

needed to get herself into a standing position.

Her hands are knots

huddled together on pink rosary beads.

Crooked, swollen fingers

take in one bead at a time

with a cadence set by lips

once young, plump, and dumb,

but now as thin and sharp

as albatross wings coming in for a landing

on a buoy in the middle of the ocean.

I've never seen or heard her up close,

but I don't think she's praying for herself.

The whole thing is too disciplined,

too focused, too entrenched a duty.

It's an act of war, an act of love.

It's a shield for the world

and the kids and grandkids who live in it.

A shield for the guy who delivers her meals,

and the beautician, who also does toenails.

It's a shield for that lady and her ugly dog,

who stop on the sidewalk

by the lilac bush every morning,

and watch through the glass door.

Guilt

A panicked grasshopper

unsuccessfully tried

to get away

from the flat end

of my sister's toy beach shovel.

She was two. I was five.

She thought she was protecting me.

I cried because I'm the one who brought the hopper.

Sometimes misunderstandings

become themes.

St. Monica

I'm cleaning out my wallet
and I pull a dog-eared prayer card
tucked between a reminder
of a year-old dentist appointment
and a folded receipt
for three bags of chicken feed.

Saint Monica. Patron of mothers.
Every time Augustine looked over his shoulder
there she was, praying
like her hair was on fire
and her son's conversion
was the only extinguisher for miles.

Poor Augustine, already weary
of the undignified, pleading tone
in notes from every priest in Thagaste.
"Please. Isn't there something you can do
about your mother? *Anything*?"

Monica cold-trailed her son
from university to bar to brothel and back,
shed prayers that could have

peeled paint off the ceiling of the Sistine Chapel
had she lived another few hundred years.

St. Augustine couldn't run fast enough.
No one can run fast enough.
St. Monica will pray for your kids, too,
and she doesn't mess around.

She found me in Montana years ago
at Emmaus Road Book Store,
roped me from across the room and
pulled me towards a swivel rack of cards.

Her likeness fell off the rack
into my hand in broad daylight,
right there in the middle
of all those crucifixes
and empty plastic bottles labeled Holy Water.
Oh sure, there were tears,
but my eye stopped twitching.

"Don't worry," she said. "We got this."

The Gardener Wants to Do Something About the Prairie Dogs

The prairie smells like fresh hope.

I ascend the steps

as someone gives the bell

in the tower a few rings.

Bulbous droplets of rain

thump like tiny sandbags

onto the bowed heads

of last year's yarrow,

soaking sagebrush weary of pushing back

on nature's cold indignities.

The morning light stretches out

over the barking heads

of a prairie dog town that sprang up

along the south lawn a year or two ago.

God's wee clown puppies,

popping in and out

of the world at will,

no choice but to spread

porous destruction

in the name of their own instincts,

oblivious

to how the rest of us can fall

into the hidden traps

of their innocent tunnels.

Not unlike me

when I thought my faith

was a given like blue eyes,

would play itself out

however it played itself out,

even if left to chance

through a dark winter—

or that wet spring,

when bean seeds rotted in the ground.

Vespers and Old Sticky Gates

Praise for the moment
I pushed the right button
on the blue tooth device.

Praise for the chanting monks
that ride along to the garden
to tuck the chickens in for the night.

Praise for this warped pole fence
that creaks psalms
when the wind blows.

Praise to you, Jesus,
for leaving my old sticky gate
jammed wide open.

Fear and Wisdom Make Eye Contact on the Sidewalk in Front of the Post Office

Their fresh reflection leans
on the spotless glass door—
newly opened purple petunias,
in an earth-colored planter
roughly the size of a cradle.

Every morning at daybreak,
Luke the maintenance man
gives them a little drink of water.

Holy water.
Made so by the pain
in his seventy five-year-old spine
as he stoops to tip the can
toward leaf and root.

Luke knows better than anyone
how hard they are trying

to bloom wide-open,

even though the wind doesn't stop for long.

He sees no need to upset them further

with stories about the upcoming hard freeze.

Instead, when they raise their anxious faces,

(See misty droplets on velvet cheeks)

he tells them,

"It's okay. Things aren't as they seem."

He tells them,

"You're passion flowers, being chanted

in a love poem that never ends."

Branding Day and the Wind is a Little Chilly

but what do I care?

Best to just pull my collar

up a bit and watch,

an old woman so proud

of the men her sons have become,

that if she turns her gratitude

up more than half a notch,

she'll burst into flames.

Keeping it Simple

You've always been here, Lord,
even when I couldn't hear you.
Even when I stumbled
through the jungle
in waist-high waders,
through inky lagoons,
under trees full of snakes,
calling your name,
searching my pockets for a map.
You're here, alright.
Even when I can't hear
over the sound of traditions
being burned alive.
Even when I trip over idiocies
with my name on them.
Even when vultures
squawk in my ear.
I plant my feet in you.
And stick.

What to do With a Blast of Cold Air, a Slick Chute of Mud

It's as worthy a topic as any,
the lilacs that bloomed early one year
outside the General Store, then,
surprised by icy air that came out of nowhere
and stayed just long enough to remind them
about the nature of impermanence,
froze stiff and fell off their happy stems.

There they lay on an uneven sidewalk
to be crunched by cowboy boots on their way
to the post office. Swept into the gutter
by cashier Hazel's broken broom,
they didn't cry a single tear,
just waited, rode the next rain right on down
through iron grates in the drain.

Came out south of town.
A smooth slide into the river
landed them on a moist bank,
where they helped
a cheerful community of worms
build a cottonwood tree.

Maybe Time and Space are Overrated

Faith shakes out a blanket that floats on the air.

I sit under it and close my eyes.

Easter Mass is about to begin.

Everybody is here in my mind.

We're taking up the whole row.

My granddaughters have been twirling

their fluffy finery all morning.

My grandson is wearing a cowboy hat.

Sons and daughters-in-law sit holding hands beside me.

Across the isle and up one row,

another lady sits alone. I open my eyes

just in time to catch the side of her face smiling.

That's how I know her family is here, too.

Poem Where I Try to Kill a Bird

I.

Romantic love isn't unlike a foreign country

you've only visited in your mind.

Grassy meadows where cows

with full udders and floral wreaths on their heads

stroll and chew.

The narrow streets are of cobblestone,

irresistible, but bumpy.

A violinist plays "Ave Maria"

somewhere in the background.

You can't see him,

but you know, you just know,

he looks like that actor

who portrays Jesus in The Chosen.

There are window boxes and striped awnings.

A book shop. A bakery.

The scent of hot bread and raw butter.

Your eyes roll back in your head

when your brain gives you a taste,

lets you wash it down with Beaujolais Nouveau

from a crystal glass.

A ten-foot fountain in the square

spews rainbows out the top of an angel's head.

II.

Don't miss Notre Dame de Paris.

A lot of ash now, but never mind that.

Enjoy the stained glass windows

that swallow light, then digest, triage,

and shoot joy and redemption

onto the shoulders

of sobbing parishioners, and tourists.

Handmade wrought-iron doors

tout a heavy squat behind an entry

arched like Zeus' mustache.

Myth has it that such beautiful work

could not have been created by human hands,

that Biscornet sold his soul to the devil

and died soon after the project was complete.

III.

Do what you want,
but I suggest you maintain as much eye contact
with the gargoyles as possible.
Their job is to deflect
erosive weather from the walls,
and more important for our purposes,
(what with their primordial brow structure,
fangs, and claws,)
to frighten and defend
against evil spirits.
From high-up, their cold orbs
scan the countryside for improprieties.
Even so, no worries
as I walk along the road
with a rolled-up street map in my hand,
swatting hard the dumb birds
that every once in a while,
fly right out of my heart.

Faith, a Dog, a Pair of New Shoes

Once all the things have been described—
the shape of a sleeping baby's mouth,
wind socks, prairie fire, and northern lights,
the specific gravity of sin
and how it rubbed-off on your sleeve
when you danced with it—
the unimportant distractions
fall-off like crumbs you've brushed
from the front of your sweater.
There goes the television,
the useless desires,
the ridiculous needs for approval.
I'm not exactly sure
where I'm going with this, but stay with me.
You'll understand better if you're old.
Something about the four cardinal directions.
The urge to tear a random hole in another one
and step through, invisible.
Only take faith, a dog, a pair of new shoes
that can handle bunions.
Find places to help someone else,
but don't tell them.
Only stop when God knocks on your door
wearing a tilted fedora and smoking a big cigar.

Got No Troubles

You'll get no lament from me,
even though goals from youth
kept dying their hair
and boarding busses to unknown locations.
I wave a wild rag
and bid each good riddance.

After church the grandkids are coming over
to improve the air and sound quality
in my cottage.

This afternoon, the dogs and I
will hike along the river.

Tonight, C.S. Lewis
is going to meet me in the bathtub.

Tomorrow morning, I'll head out
to plant flowers all over
my garden-the-size-of-a-cemetery.

Thanks for asking.

The Death of St. Joseph

One foot in a shack, one in a mansion,
doesn't matter, either way.
He listens to Mary's soft sobs,
surprised by them.
He'd always imagined himself
the one blessed, the one content
to watch them from the background,
make sure they were safe, fed, loved.
A poor carpenter could offer no more.
Now, she is weeping over him.
And his boy, by his side, assuring safe passage.
He was glad he hadn't seen himself
through their eyes until now.
It might have changed something.

—The inspiration for this ekphrastic poem is Giuseppe
Maria Crespi's painting, The Death of St. Joseph, circa 1712.

ACKNOWLEDGEMENTS

—Oceans of gratitude to my loves, Sandy, Morgan, Penny, Lindsey, Oakley, Emory Bell, Addison, Dusty, and Tierney, for being the blessings and joys of my life.

—Thank you to my publisher, Ryan Collins of Powder River Publishing, for giving this book an opportunity, and for your endless patience and encouragement.

Grateful acknowledgment is made to the editors of the following publications where a few of these poems originally appeared, sometimes in a different form:

Heart of Flesh Literary Journal

Macrina Magazine: Fresh Philosophical Engagements With an Ancient Faith

Spirit Fire Review

Imogene's Notebook on Medium

Unbroken Journal

ABOUT THE AUTHOR

Lyndi Waters is the author of *Butcher Shop of Wild Forgiveness* (2021). She is a winner of the Frank Nelson Doubleday Memorial Writing Award, the Eugene V. Shea National Poetry Contest, and is a repeat winner of the Wyoming Writers, Inc. competition in poetry and flash fiction. Lyndi is a Pushcart Prize nominee (Picaroon Poetry, U.K.). Her work has been published in numerous literary journals and anthologies, including Blood, Water, Wind, and Stone: An Anthology of Wyoming Writers (Sastrugi Press, 2016). Lyndi lives in Wyoming.